A Bright Light For A Beautiful Soul

A Bright Light For A Beautiful Soul

Hikeem Wallace

"You are going to have the light just a little while longer. Walk while you have the light, before darkness overtakes you. Whoever walks in the dark does not know where they are going. Believe in the light, so that you may become children of light."

— John 12:35-36 NIV

Acknowledgments

My gratitude to everyone who graciously spoke words of encouragement that equipped me for this journey. I would be remiss if I did not acknowledge many thanks to everyone who prayed for me during this process. Your presence was felt and helped carry me through the finished line. My hat is tipped and my heart expresses a huge thank you.

A major thank you goes out to my editor and tremendous friend, Ms. Zenitha Brown. You have worked tirelessly in helping me to perfect this book. You are a true blessing to the Kingdom.

Special thanks to my visual and creative artist, Mr. Antwan Twizzy Campbell, who designed and developed the book cover.

I would like to thank Ms. Erika Buffaloe and Mr. Chris Johnson for their technical support and contribution to this book.

Introduction

As human beings, we are always in the process of becoming. The mind gets its marching orders from the heart, which is the seat of our emotions. The mind begins to survey the landscape for purpose. It is that passion for a purpose that moves the needle from us being dormant to living, to moving and to having our being. This directive affirms the neediness of man for God's presence. If we start from the beginning, we will discover that God created man as a volitional being to think and make rational decisions based on many characteristics of Himself. Therefore, man has the freedom to choose which direction he wants to walk in: either obedience to God or allegiance to the world system. Here is man's dilemma, since man lives in the world, his greater influence is the one that insulates his surroundings and illustrates how to do it. So, man will always find himself torn and tattered because the world does not have the answers to man's many tough questions.

What is needed is a mediator that will shine His spotlight on man and redirect his heart back to the person of God.

> Jesus said, *"I am the light of the world, Whoever follows me will never walk in darkness, but will have the light of life."*
>
> — *(John 8:12 NIV)*

This is a compelling statement, for Jesus makes the affirmation that those who follow Him will always walk in the light. To walk in the light is to have clarity and concise insights into the mind of God, which will help us make better decisions. This is pivotal when it comes to money and the stewardship of it. The scripture tells us that God gives Man the power and provisions to get wealth; therefore, making money is not an evil act.

> *But remember the Lord your God, for it is he who gives you the ability to produce wealth.*
>
> — *(Deuteronomy 8:18a NIV)*

The prevailing view is whatever gift God places in the hands of man cannot be evil but it becomes evil when that gift takes on a higher value in our heart than the Giver of it. This is the struggle for the rich young ruler, who gravitates to the tangible assets that dominate his heart and eventually wants to master his soul. Whenever we replace God with any person, any place and anything, it severs our relationship with the one who created us. Adulatory is God's kryptonite. It breaks His heart. But the God of everything is like the hound of Heaven. He will chase and chase after you to bring you back home to fulfill your divine purpose.

This is the good news; God uses the *Bright Light* to reprogram and; to reactivate the heart of man to usher him back to His presence and His power to do the miraculous. Using the storylines of Abram and Judas, you will see that God looks at each of us through the lens of oneness and being connected to Him in the relationship of fatherhood. This is where God oversees our footprints and leads us to the fertile ground where we will become fruitful if our faith prevails. But in His sovereign nature, God gives us the individuality to explore a life that does not dictate what He decrees. The twists and turns in the life of the rich young ruler are integrated through the challenges that we all face when trying to please God and also satisfy our souls.

A Bright Light For A Beautiful Soul

Have you ever had an encounter with someone who just amazed you? They had an inviting spirit, one that made you want to root for them to come out on the winning side. They had a magnanimous personality which manifested a change in any room. The words that fell from their lips were edifying and always encouraging; so that when you left their presence, you were empowered to walk bolder and with much more conviction. Their background was laced with powerful testimonies of how they overcame trying times in a triumphant way. They were always armed with a prayer in their back pocket, for they believed in the power of God reaching down from heaven to make a way. Some would call this person a beautiful soul, a person who exudes kindness. A bright light that is full of good intentions. Past generations would call this person an old soul, one that holds firm to traditions and the teaching from those who carried out the imprint of those experiences. Suppose we would examine the good deeds of this dynamic person and attach them to the intent of why they were carried out. Would their works meet God's requirement to receive eternal life? Before you answer, Dr. R. C. Sproul put it this way, "One concept to consider is the law of cosmic order which states that we are always compensated for what we do." The word *compensation* is defined as being rewarded or redeeming what was lost.

When it comes to the economy of God, we all have received a bonus benefit. God takes the liberty to provide the resources so that man is never left without; therefore, he can win the day. It is the providence of God that goes before us and prepares us to have success. Likewise, our faith to believe and obtain salvation is borrowed from God.

> *For by grace are you saved through faith; and that not of yourselves:*
> *it is a gift of God.*
>
> *— Ephesians 2:8 KJV*

What the Apostle Paul is communicating is that faith is required for us to dwell in God's presence; but in reality, it is a faith that is not ours but God's. The prophet Habakkuk warns us that he whose soul is lifted up shall perish but one who trusts in God by faith shall live. The word *live* is implied to getting the care by a special means. In this case, God is man's procurer.

Abram's Faithfulness

Let's consider the life of Abram, which was marked by obedience, for he sacrificed family, finance and familiarity to walk with God.

> Now the LORD had said unto Abram, *"Get thee out of thy country and from thy kindred and from thy father's house, unto a land that I will shew thee."*

> — *Genesis 12:1 KJV*

Let us examine the difficulty of leaving your family behind. Sociologists for the past decade have screamed out that the family is the fabric of stabilizing a healthy society. The support of parents plays a significant role in the shaping and molding of a child's development and in their decision-making. The separation of the father and or the mother can cause an increase in sadness, anxiety, fear, and various behavior problems. It can lead to signs of dysfunction and disillusion that can linger into the third and fourth generations. Abraham also sacrificed wealth.

And Abram was very rich in cattle, in silver, and in gold.

— Genesis 13:2 KJV

The stability of having financial freedom is an asset. It allows you to produce and provide. It opens doors for you to walk through what only the privileged have access to. It gives you credit lines that will enable you to make essential and non-essential purchases. It gives you the freedom to take advantage of investing in great opportunities and most of all, it is a segue to avoid debt.

What about familiarity? This is a hot topic that we do not often talk about. The price of being comfortable is a luxury that we enjoy but the effort to get it is often overlooked.

And Lot also, which went with Abram, had flocks, and herds, and tents. And the land was not able to bear them, that they might dwell together: for their substance was great, so that they could not dwell together.

— Genesis 13:5,6 KJV

Your faith in making uncomfortable sacrifices in unfamiliar territory oftentimes can put you in a cumbersome position. Abraham took his nephew Lot along for the journey to this unknown land that the LORD had commissioned him to go to. In their travels, they discovered that there was just too much commerce between the two parties to survive together; Abram, being the good soul, offered his nephew the choice of dwelling: a lush and plush pasture or the dry and dusty desert.

Judas Financial Hunger

The Holy Bible often speaks about God wanting His children to live an abundant life. What if the desire is driven or motivated by money? We know that money is not the root of evil and if we are good stewards of what God places in our hands, that can only bring glory, honor and adoration to God. Using Judas Iscariot as a case study for one who desired the feel of money, we can suggest that riches can be a stumbling block for one's desired end in the eyes of God. The introduction to Judas Iscariot is immediately met with a crucial question mark, for the scripture tells us that Judas was selected to be one of Jesus's disciples. However, he gave him a tagline of the betrayer. Now the names of the twelve disciples are these; The first is Simon, who is called Peter, and Andrew his brother; James the son of Zebedee, and John his brother; Philip, and Bartholomew; Thomas, and Matthew the publican; James the son of Alphaeus, and Lebbaeus, whose surname was Thaddaeus; Simon the Canaanite, and Judas Iscraiot, who also betrayed him.(Matthew 10:2-4 KJV)What raises a question from this scripture is that Judas is the only one with his full name disclosed. The name Iscraiot comes from Latin, and it means *leather bag*, although this could refer to the leather bag that he always had draped over his shoulders.

For some of them thought, because Judas had the bag, that Jesus has said unto him,

"Buy those things that we have need of against the feast or that he should give something to the poor."

— John 13:29 KJV

In addition to this trademark of him carrying a bag, we see the indictment of him being a thief. This he said, not that he cared for the poor; but because he was a thief and had the bag and bare what was put therein." (John 12:6 KJV) As I reflect on my life and my duplicitous behavior, I can say that I also carried that leather bag as I robbed Jesus of His reverence and honor as my Lord and Savior.

The myriad of moments that I sat at the throne of my heart instead of offering that seat to the Master to rest and to rule, which was a result of my dependency on walking without the authority of God. The decisions of Judas' downfall, oftentimes like many of us, start with a thought that enters our soul and germinates into an action. Here is how the gospel of Matthew puts it: Judas was called to be one of Jesus's disciples (Matthew 10:4); Judas went to the chief priest to deliver up Jesus (Matthew 26:14,15); Judas is promised thirty pieces of silver (Matthew 26:15); Judas comes with a great multitude with swords and staves to take Jesus prisoner (Matthew 26:47 NJK); Judas confessed that he has betrayed innocent blood (Matthew 27:4 KJV); Judas returned the thirty pieces of silver (Matthew 27:5); and finally Judas commits suicide. (Matthew 27:5 KJV) Words to live by; your actions today can be the platform for problems tomorrow. In the case of Judas, money monopolized his motives to live an unfruitful life for the Father.

God Has A Purpose And A Plan

If ever there was something so dear to your heart, to me, it would be knowing the plan that God has purposed in your heart. God's plan for you is to be with Him spiritually as well as physically. Therefore, God will do whatever it takes to protect and preserve your life with His promise to take us with Him. Jesus said I will go and prepare a place for you, and I will come back and take you to be with me that you also may be where I am. (John 14:3 NIV) In the person of Abraham, it was to build him in faith that would move the mountain of doubt, and for Judas, it was to know the character and the commands of God. The character of God is found in His attributes, which come under the umbrella of His love. The immutable attributes of the Sovereign God are not swayed by any circumstances or conditions that impregnate man's heart. The Lord is consistent and He has a purpose for everything that He does. The scripture teaches us that God always does that which is good. His lovingkindness is always on display, and it delivers manifold blessings.

But God demonstrates His own love toward us, in that while we were still sinners, Christ died for us.

— Romans 5:8 NASB

The Greek Septuagint reads; as God loved us, even when we were no use to Him. In the case of Abram and Judas, the Lord uses each man to manifest the desired outcome that will fulfill His divine purpose. In the sacrifices of Abram, God walked with him in the good and in the difficult times; so that the moments did not get overwhelming for him. For example, the Abrahamic Covenant, which covers four chapters (Genesis 12, 13, 15, and 17), is an unconditional agreement between God and Abram. The traditional covenant was the picture of the two parties walking together between two pieces of a sacrificed animal, showing they would abide by the conditions of the contract. In this covenant, God, in His sovereign nature, decided that He alone would walk between the two pieces of the sacrificed animal, expressing that He would put no conditions on Abram to have this covenant come to fruition. As you read through the scriptures, you will see that God often shoulders the burden; He takes the liberty and the ownership to ensure that His plan will always go forth with expectancy, not leaving it to chance with man. However, Judas conquest to feed his flesh and to starve his soul took on the character of disobedience without true repentance.

His final act of a remorseful soul was a useless passion that did not profit his eternal destination. At such a time, Judas coveted with the religious leaders of that day to betray Jesus for thirty pieces of silver. But when his conscience became clear of the righteousness of God, these same men dismissed the tenderness of his heart and they had to press him into committing this heinous act. How far is this from the loving nature of God, the one who loves on us even in the season of disobedience?

One of the Jewish customs was for the master of the ceremony to share the dipping of the bread with one he wanted to celebrate. In the sacred moments of the last supper, Jesus makes Judas the guest of honor to rear him back into the fold as a disciplined disciple. (Matthew 26:23) However, when the heart is inflamed with compassion, the season of remorse often comes too late; when the callousness of the heart is thick-skinned and is not easily penetrated, even with the grace of God. The scripture tells us that Judas proceeded forth according to what was prophesied and carried out this evil act of delivering Jesus to His adversaries. So, Judas, in the act of revenge, threw the thirty pieces of silver into the temple, where only the priest had the authority to go get it. This would signify by retrieving the silver coins that the blood would be on their hands. You can intentionally seek to do good but without the change in your disposition, the flesh will be the driving force that will earmark your efforts for a bad outcome.

Yet it pleased the LORD to bruise him; he hath put him to grief: when thou shalt make his soul an offering for sin.

— *Isaiah 53:10a KJV*

However, the sin of Judas was placed in the hands of God, and He turned it into a redeeming work that gave all of mankind the opportunity to partake of such a great salvation. As Christians, we can take comfort in the providence of God, for He takes our errors and our erroneous mistakes; and produces a finished work for His glory.

A Question From The Beautiful Soul

We have entered the age and the arena whereby asking a question does not cast a shadow on you as being labeled as unknowledgeable or beneath the realm of being an intellectual. John says to Jackie, "How do you feel?" In this question, we have an inquiry where the reply would not be a definitive answer but one that fluctuates from person to person according to their emotion. However, in many circles, asking a question adds to the degree of one showing an invested interest in the subject that is being entertained. On one occasion, while Jesus was teaching the multitude, a young man yelled out from the crowd asking the Lord to use His authority to tell his brother to share his inheritance. So, the question asked was not to gain insight into a certain topic; but into its concerned ability. Oftentimes asking a question helps bring a resolve to how we will approach our next important step.

The gospel writer John Mark, writes about a young rich ruler who came to Jesus asking one of the most important questions that could ever be asked. Before the question is asked, Mark gives us some insight by describing this man's passion and his posture. He comes to Jesus running and then bowing down. In the culture of that day, men wore long robes and underneath was their tunic. The tunic was an undergarment that was seamless and sleeveless that came down to the knees. It would be like today, a woman wearing a slip under her dress, giving protection to the body from the outer garment. So, to run in this attire was not a picture of comfort. His determination speaks volumes about the validity and efficacy of this question. The scripture tells us that upon approaching Jesus, he knelt, demonstrating humility and acknowledging his desperate need to find satisfaction. The rich young ruler did not come asking a question of how to get more money nor how to increase his social status but to get an answer that had a weightier value. This man wanted to get confirmation that appealed to his lifestyle and, at the same time, get God's approval. As a side note, something that is never discussed when we entertain this conversation between Jesus and the rich ruler is the favor that is shown to this young man. Favor is something done or granted out of goodwill rather than from justice or for remuneration. Favor helps you to skip levels by leaping over required steps which pushes you closer to your desired expectation. In the spiritual realm, this man was endowed with much favor by God, which allowed him to come face to face with the omniscient one to ask an ontological question. Just a few minutes earlier, the scriptures tell us that little children were being denied the opportunity to come to Jesus by his disciples. (Mark 10:13 KJV) However, somehow this man pushed through the crowd and was granted by God to have a solo conversation with the Savior.

The Most Important Questions
Ever Asked

Have you ever heard a lecture and afterward had a burning question that inflamed your spirit and captivated your thoughts continuously? The very thought of asking this question made your nerves rattle because the importance of addressing this question with clarity and using the correct verbiage haunted you. This man came out of the gate with perfect footing; he called Jesus, "Good Master." The New International Version reads, "Good teacher," the title given to Him as one teaching with great authority.

For He taught them as one having authority, and not as the scribes.

— Matthew 7:29 KJV

The rich young ruler standing tall and poised, said to Jesus, "What shall I do that I may inherit eternal life?" On the surface, I am sure this man was waiting for a long list of requirements and regulations that the Master would pronounce he had to follow. But Jesus remained still and with a quieted spirit must have pondered this man's question, for the structure of his question, speaks of something that he had not earned.

The words "to inherit" implies taking possession of something as your right. The more appropriate words from the rich ruler would have been "to gain." To gain refers to acquiring possession of something that you never had before. Digging a little deeper, the theological import puts emphasis on something that the rich man must do versus the complete work of the atonement by Christ. This makes you wonder if this man fell asleep doing some of the teachings from Jesus, for He often spoke of His death to save the world.

Verily, verily, I say unto you, Except a corn of wheat fall into the ground and die, it abideth alone: but if it die, it bringeth forth much fruit.

— John 12:24 KJV

I believe this is one reason why pastors can say; they can preach the same sermon several times and many will not know it. But I give credit to where credit is due. This man deposited in his spirit the climatic part of Jesus's teaching. He had listening ears when it came to hearing about eternal life.

The subject of eschatology is intriguing to every believer who embraces life after death. It is the science of the last things and, for the Christian, the destiny of the soul. The fabric of knowing that future information can tug at the heart and mind, specifically when it culminates with the plans of God. Jesus, on many occasions, gave some insight into the illumination of God's messianic plan and how they were manifested in the parables.

He answered and said unto them, because it is given unto you to know the mysteries of the kingdom of heaven.

— Matthew 13:11a KJV

When the New Testament speaks of eschatology, it is concerned with physical death and spiritual life, heaven and hell and the second coming of Christ. If I could take the liberty to survey what was going on in this man's mind, I believe his heart was concerned with where his soul would be after his death.

Placing Our Eyes On Jesus

Let's take our eyes off the rich man and place it on the character of Jesus. As you read through the scriptures, you will find some man or woman, some leader or lay person, some believer or non-believer would come to Jesus with a question and He would reply to that person in the structure of a question. Let's be clear, Jesus was not asking the question because what He heard was too difficult for Him to answer. In essence, Jesus uses the structure of asking a rhetorical question so that the person would recall information that they already know. Jesus says to this man, "Why do you call me good?' There is none good but one, that is God." (Mark 10:18) As a Jew, this man would have been taught by his parents that the God of Abraham, Isaac and Jacob was the only good and perfect Being in this universe.

And these words, which I command thee this day, shall be in thin heart: And thou shall teach them diligently unto thy children.

— Deuteronomy 6:6-7a KJV

Because the Bible is written in the redemptive form and is structured with revelatory insights, it would behoove us to not think that Jesus was questioning this man to see where he was in his theology. This is not the first time that Jesus puts man to the test when it comes to His classification or title. When Jesus was with His disciples in Caesarea Philippi, after healing a deaf-mute, He said to His disciples, "Who do men say that I am?" The answers came in the form of John the Baptist, Elias, or one of the other prophets. (Mark 8:27-28 KJV) Jesus then probed a little deeper and asked for their opinion and here we get the great confession of Peter, You are the Christ. (Mark 8:29 KJV) A question to ponder is, what is the importance of disciples knowing Jesus's title? Followers of Christ need to have a deeper appreciation of the one who came to save them from their sins before they can understand the pathway that leads to their salvation. What Jesus was looking for was the answer that flowed from a regenerated heart and a renewed mind. The word regeneration comes from the Greek word *romanized,* which refers to a rebirth. It is a spiritual metamorphosis that takes place when the callus heart is changed to one that is now made of flesh and yields to the things of God. The renewed mind, according to the Apostle Paul, is to think contrary to the world by having the rationale to embrace God's good and perfect will. The Astronomer Johannes Kepler gives it a little flavor with his quote on how we should approach life: "Thinking God's thoughts after Him." Unfortunately, if we read between the lines, we will see that this man had a superficial view of eternal life and the person of Jesus Christ.

The Church Declaration Of Jesus As God

After the death of Jesus Christ, the Church was inundated with many questions and few answers to give to the believer. These questions ranged from the teaching of first-century apostles to how to celebrate the Passover. The biggest controversy was the nature of Jesus Christ. In 325 AD, a group of 318 bishops came together to the city of Bithynian in Nicaea, modern-day Turkey, to give their declaration under the Roman Emperor Constantine, affirming the deity of Christ. This was important because it brought together all the competing views of the nature of Jesus. Just as a side note, out of this ecumenical council, they gave a mandate for a uniform day to commemorate Easter. Just as we experience wrestling and wrangling with the masses to accept and conform in the 21st century, the 4th century was not foreign to this struggle. In 450 AD, another council of 520 bishops came together in a city called Chalcedon, near Asia Minor, to discuss the Incarnation of Jesus.

This council finalized and put to rest the church's view of the two natures of Christ: that Jesus is fully Man and fully God. The theological term often used is the hypostatic union of God. These two councils give us some insights into what the earlier Christians struggled with, along with this rich young ruler. To identify Jesus simply as a good teacher and one who speaks with great wisdom falls way short of knowing Him as the God of everything. If you take away the deity of Jesus, we are left with a good man who has no power to save us, nor Himself. How comforting it is to know that Christ Jesus has the power to create something out of nothing and to bring life out of death. It was so important for the leaders of the Christian faith to get this right at this pivotal time in history; for it was the foundation by which the church would stand or fall.

The Law

One way of legislating a domain where joy, peace and love are at the forefront of keeping a healthy relationship between Man and God is to set in place guidelines or rules. As a child living in my parent's home, I was taught that certain rules were set in place to govern the peace of the house. The rules did not change according to age or gender but they were the same for everyone to obey. If we all followed the rules, there would be harmony in the home; if one was indifferent to the rules, there would be disorder. God is the greatest parent of them all, so likewise, He put some rules in place; let's call them commandments. The commandments are not suggestions but they are legislation that divinely orders this universe to meet God's satisfaction. The first five are focused on our relationship with God and the second group of five is set in place to help us enjoy the relationship with each other. In Exodus 20:3-17, we have the written law, which is referred to as the *Ten Commandments*, also known as the *Decalogue*, which means ten words. In total, there are 613 laws, which we find in the Mishnah and the Jewish Talmud. The Mishnah was the oral interpretation and the first written collection of the law that the Hebrew people were to adhere to, while the Jewish Talmud was a collection of writings from the rabbis getting the understanding of how to apply the law. Now if we examine the purpose of the law, we will see that it does not have the efficacy nor the pervasiveness to relinquish the punishment of sin.

All who sin apart from the law will also perish apart from the law, and all who sin under the law will be judged by the law.

— Romans 2:12 NIV

Jesus's Reply

After hearing the rich young ruler's question, Jesus replied, You know the commandments: You shall not murder, you shall not commit adultery, you shall not steal, you shall not give false testimony, you shall not defraud, honor your father and your mother. (Mark 10:19 NIV) The first thing that jumps out is this man's nationality. He was of Jewish descent, for the Jew was connected to God by His covenant and was taught at an early age to worship this monotheistic God. The parents were giving examples of how to diligently teach their children: by talking with them as they are sitting in the house, using frontlets before their eyes and writing this information on the door post in the home. So, Jesus reminds this man at the outset, obeying God's law is the premise for anyone receiving eternal life. Why? Because the law sets an orderly account of how to love God and man. Love is the core attribute of who God is. And it encompasses His attributes of omniscience, omnipotence, omnipresence and God's immutability. Now there are different degrees of love that are spelled out in the Greek language, such as *agape, philia and eros,* just to name a few. *Agape* is the highest form of love, which is demonstrated by God. *Philia* is a sacrificial love that puts others ahead of themselves. It is the action of a brother providing for another brother or sister. It is the picture of someone showing affection that goes much deeper than human emotions. *Eros* is the love that is seen between a married man and a married woman. It comes into the English language as erotic, a sensual desire or appetite for their spouse. *Agape* is seen as the greatest form of love, for it has the action of giving something away, while *eros is* classified in a lower tier; for it is self-seeking. Jesus, whom we stated earlier, was affirmed by the church in the council of Nicaea and the council of Chalcedon as being fully man and, at the same time, fully God, has the knowledge of knowing this man's heart. Jesus directs this man to the second half of the table of the Ten Commandments, which deals with the love displayed toward his neighbor. At first glance, it seems odd that Jesus would bypass the commands that relate to God, for we are told that to reverence God was the greatest of all the laws.

> *And Jesus answered him, "The first of all the commandments is, Hear O Israel; The Lord our God is one Lord: And thou shalt love the Lord thy God with all thy heart, and with all thy soul and with all thy mind, and with all thy strength."this is the first commandment." (Mark 12:29-30 KJV)*

Once again, the scripture brings light to our clouded thinking, for the author of Hebrews tells us that God's ways are different from our ways and they always provide a greater purpose. Jesus uses the relationship with our neighbor first because no human being has ever loved God with all their heart, their mind or their strength. Second, human experiences work better with people that we can see and touch. I am sure by now, the critics of the Christian community are pointing out that Jesus is throwing His hat in the ring and affirming that human works are tied to your salvation. Before you roll your sleeves up and want to have a physical debate, I believe that Jesus is using this tactic to produce the knowledge of the law to show this man the error of his ways. If we are honest, we can look at this list and weep; for we know that we have broken one or all these commandments. Here is where the beauty of God's love emanates from the darkest place where we stand.

For all have sinned, and come short of the glory of God. Being justified freely by His grace through the redemption that is in Christ Jesus.

— Romans 3:23-24 KJV

What the Apostle Paul is communicating to us is that we all have fallen short of God's expectations as creatures that He has shaped and molded in His likeness. But the good news is that we have an advocate that has interceded on our behalf, Christ Jesus, who is fully man and fully God.

A Superficial View Of The Law

After the rich young ruler got the explanation from Jesus concerning what is needed to have eternal life, he must have breathed a deep sigh of relief. I am sure that he thought to himself, that is all! The rich young ruler then began to justify himself by saying, "Teacher," he declared, "all these I have kept since I was a boy." (Mark 10:20 NIV) What a beautiful soul! The text gives us the feeling that this man was still under the delusion that if he could keep all the commandments, then God would welcome him into the kingdom. He still struggled with the notion of works as the means to justification. Here is the question that I would raise to this man: What if you broke one of the commandments in the days ahead; what would be your plan to regain that salvation that you worked so hard to obtain? This is the beauty of the Christian faith; your salvation is not based on you but on the complete and finished work of Christ. This means that God's requirements were satisfied in Christ Jesus, who is fully man and fully God. He took the universal route of doing something that no man could do, which was to gain enough righteousness so that it could be applied to all humanity. To give this statement some clarity, man is bankrupt in righteousness and does not have the spiritual aptitude to gain it. St. Augustine said, our greatest works are nothing but splendid vices in the eyes of God. We must remember that the works that we deem to be good are not seen side by side with our neighbor, but are measured up against the righteousness of our Holy God. This is what Martin Luther, the father of the *Reformation Movement*, had to learn from his earlier years in the monastery. I believe the rich ruler was taking a page out of Martin Luther's playbook. Luther's philosophical plan was to be the monk of all monks from his sacrifices and his studying God's word. To Luther, it was all about performance and the diligence to please God. Just as human performance does not meet perfection, the law was not meant to be the savior of the world; but it was to show us how far off we are from the requirements of God.

Missing the Mark

What is puzzling is that this man never once mentioned his affection for God. His attention was solely focused on what he could get from the hand of God. Many of us are the same way. We come to God without any praise or worship unto Him. We overlook His face and jump right into granting my petition. When David, the anointed and soon-appointed king, found himself in trouble, he said, "I will extol the LORD at all times, and his praise will always be on my lips." (Psalm 34:1 NIV) We, too, need to embrace the idea of engaging the monotonous. It is important to express our love for God, for He inhabits our praise. There will never be anyone who loves you more than the Lord God. What man would surrender his life for you? The Apostle Paul speaks of Jesus being our propitiator. He is the one that takes our place in receiving the wrath, the punishment from God.

Whom God hath set forth to be a propitiation through faith in his blood, to declare his righteousness for the remission of sins that are past, through the forbearance of God.

— Romans 3:25 KJV

What Paul is saying is that Christ Jesus is the object of our faith, not just His crucifixion. But everything that He did is a complete work of redemption. The blood of Jesus is what was paid. In layman's terms, Jesus did the heavy lifting while we watched and we became the beneficiaries of His labor. We live in a world where people would rather chase after capital than seek after Christ. Their confidence is in the tangible assets, not the faith that can turn a mustard seed into a magnificent blessing. How the unregenerate mind lacks understanding. If you get Christ Jesus, you get everything. He is your *Jehovah Shalom*, the God of your peace; *Jehovah Jireh*, the God who provides; *Jehovah Rappa* , the God who heals; *Jehovah Shammah*, the God who walks with and talks with you. Jesus desires to have an intimate relationship with you. The rich ruler missed the mark and lost the treasures of having Jesus as his friend.

Greater love has no one than this: to lay down one's life for one's friend. You are my friends if you do what I command. Instead, I have called you friends, for everything that I learned from my Father I have made know to you.

— John 15:13-15 NIV

Growing up, I often heard the saying that it is a tough world out there. The seeds that were being sown in my spirit were that you need to make as many friends as you can. They would follow that saying with, "A friend shows himself to be friendly." The implication was that your actions were the love language of this call. The word *philoi* is the ancient Greek word for friend. It refers to the concept of reciprocity, a mutual exchange between two or more people. If the advice that I was hearing was true, then a friendship with Jesus is something that no person should want to pass up. I can stop right here and testify that my walk with Jesus has fortified me with the faith to face my tomorrows. I indeed trust Him for everything.

Misguided and Miscues

What shapes a person's thinking and how it is seen through the works of their hand? Some would say it is the outer workings of their environment. What they see being manifested in their mind is the segue to success. Many would say it is bred through tradition. The culture mandates it on its people. Others take the path of trial and error, finding the answers through their life experiences. This all points to those espousing their ideas to be careful that the information spewed from their lips is correct and credible. The Apostle Paul writes to Timothy, giving him instructions on how to lead after he is gone. Paul warns him of leaders having swerved from the truth and turning to vain jangling, neither understanding what they say nor whereof they affirm it. It is essential for one's audience to not only have ears to hear but to research what is being communicated. Jesus is listening to the rich young ruler and sees that he does not have the full import of the law. This man might have had his master's degree in business education; but when it came to grasping God's commandments, his response was shaky at best. Like many of us, we repeat what we hear and affirm it like it is doctrine without any briefs of documentation. This man said yes to Jesus, "Teacher," he declared, "all these I have kept since I was a boy." (Mark 10:20 NIV) The King James Version uses the word *observed* to speak of this man's actions. So, the man could have meant that he recognized God's law since he was a boy; but the following verse gives us a clear indication that he felt comfortable in obeying them. I would think at this point in the discussion, this man would have taken the position of sitting at Jesus's feet to hear of His many parables. One of the many teachings from Jesus that fascinates me comes from the Beatitudes. In this teaching, Jesus shows us that the weightiness of scripture can be complex. For example, when Jesus begins to explain the broader view of murder or to kill, He comes from the vantage point of us walking in the flesh without knowing the repercussions. Jesus says if we are angry with our brother without a just cause, that is murder. Jesus says if we call our neighbor *Raca*, we are putting ourselves in danger of judgment. The Greek word *Raca* comes over to us in English as an empty *one*. Do you see the logic here? To say that another human being is entirely useless is also an indictment of the person of God. Genesis 1:26 says that we were made in the image of God. It is the Greek word *Imago Dei* that refers to the unique relationship between God and man. So, is God comfortable having a relationship with someone who is useless? The Holy Bible teaches us that everything that is connected to God has a purpose. Jesus also says that if we call another person a fool, then we are in danger of hellfire.

The language in the Bible is difficult to understand, especially if you come to it from the ideology of a world conscience.

> *But the natural man receiveth not the things of the Spirit of God: for they are foolish unto him: neither can he know them, because they are spiritually discerned.*
>
> *— 1 Corinthians 2:14 KJV*

What this man lacked was tempering his answer according to the spirit man inside of him. Jesus could have just said, Sir, you have broken the law ever since you left your bed this morning. Job, contrary to the rich ruler, was considered by God the most just man to walk on this earth in his day, so maybe Job could have made a case for himself to have obeyed the law completely. But the scripture tells us that he laid sacrifices daily for him and his family just in case one might have sinned. (Job 1:5 KJV)

The Tenderness Of The Savior

There are times in our life when we see the error of our ways and all that is required is a quick U-turn to cleanse our souls of the wrongdoings. There are also times when the touch of the Savior is needed to bring healing to the situation. After Jesus heard the words of the rich ruler, who spoke with great fervor about him keeping all the law, Jesus just loved on him. In the moment of correction, a tender touch can go much further than the lambasting and loud talking that crushes a person's spirit. Jesus can really read a room and He saw the heart of this man, who at this moment did not need counseling but some consoling. Just to shut the mouths of the critics of Christianity, the Lord is sovereign and He is not obligated to explain His actions.

There are times recorded in the Bible when Jesus does something so rare that it screams for an explanation and the scriptures remain silent. In Mark 8:22-26, we get the recording of Jesus restoring a blind man's sight. In this narrative, Jesus took an unusual approach to bring about his healing. All the miracles done before by Jesus were in the form of speaking a word to the situation or the laying on of hands. In this case, Jesus applied a substance to induce healing and to add to the departure of the norm. This miracle was done in stages.

Now does this mean that this man's health issue was more difficult than the others? Therefore, Jesus was overwhelmed in trying to rectify his deficiency. Not at all. There are times in the economy of God when He reserves to not reveal to us the cause and the effect. But in this case, the scripture points out that Jesus was demonstrating to this man the part where he fell short. What the rich ruler was professing to have kept, he had ministered to him by Jesus. The rich ruler neglected to demonstrate love in his relationship with his neighbor. The Apostle Paul said that there are three elements that are eternal: faith, hope and love; but the greatest of them all is love. (1 Corinthians 13:13 NLT)

Man's Insufficiency To Satisfy God

Feeling the warmth and the love of Jesus gives you that empowering spirit that you can conquer the world. His presence encompasses any fear that is dangling over your dreams and aspirations. I believe that this man was feeling pretty good about himself and was waiting for Jesus to hand him his reserved ticket to have a seat in Abraham's bosom. But Jesus says to him, "One thing you lack." Hearing these stinging words deflated the air that this man was caught up in. There is an insufficiency. The word insufficiency comes over from the Greek language to mean a shortage or inadequacy. This speaks to man's inability to meet the required task. The demands by God to satisfy His wrath due to the sins of man is a difficult task at best. It requires the death of something to purge away the evil act that was committed. This object to be sacrificed had to be holy and pure. It could not be something that was just hanging around, where we would pick it up in a cavalier way and give it to God.

In this case, Jesus was leading the rich man down the road of an internal sacrifice of self. One of the hardest things to do is to deposit in your spirit a mindset of depreciating value from oneself. Oftentimes, we set ourselves up on a pedestal with many steps so that we are elevated above our peers. The rich young ruler had to develop a new way of thinking in order for him to depart from his selfish desires and the fancies that fed his flesh. Dying to the manifestations of the world and now set apart to be used by God in whatever way the Lord saw fit.

For we are His workmanship, created in Christ Jesus unto good works, which God hath before ordained that we should walk in them.

— Ephesians 2:10 KJV

Rejecting The Word Of God

Time must have stood still as the man waited with bated breath to hear Jesus finish his sentence. Whenever we wait for a *rhema* word that has the effect of being life-altering, it has the label of eternity attached to it.

> Jesus says to the rich ruler, *"Go, sell everything you have and give to the poor, and you will have treasure in heaven. Then come, follow me."*
>
> — *Mark 10:21b NIV*

Mark, the writer of this gospel, does not want us to read into the idea that Jesus was using the concept of money as the selling point for him to win salvation. We know that the entry of walking through those pearly gates cannot be bought, for no man nor woman has God in their pocket. But in the process of receiving the hand of God, one must acknowledge that they are indeed a sinner. True repentance is a necessary act for a believer to receive God's forgiveness and His blessings.

This rich ruler had to see that he did not keep all the laws required by God. So, Jesus used the concept of money, which was this man's god, to show him that he violated the very first commandment.

Thou shalt have no other gods before Me.

— Exodus 20:3 KJV

In addition, this man also neglected to keep the five commandments that Jesus mentioned to him at the outset: do not commit adultery, do not kill, do not steal, do not bear false witness and defraud not. (Mark 10:19 KJV) The departure of money is a curse word to many of us, for it is that tangible resource that represents our value. It marks our status in society and the affluence that we have amongst our peers. It is the primary entity that allows us to purchase goods and services that provides a level of comfort that separates us from our neighbor. Money creates an invisible power in the mind of man, for it gives him the freedom to make decisions without weighing the consequences before it is uploaded in real-time. It speaks to one's achievements, good stewardship and profitable investments. Let me awaken you to the truth. Sowing into your neighbor is also a good investment.

Those who give to the poor will lack nothing, but those who close their eyes to them receive many curses.

— Proverbs 28:27 KJV

Just think, this man was prospering daily while many in his community were in shambles in search of their next provisions. However, you might not get the same type of return; your eternal account will be significantly increased. When we think of it theologically, it is a small price to pay for what God has invested in us.

Missing Heaven's Treasures

So far, this rich ruler has failed every test that was put on him and now is the time for his redemption. Jesus tells him to sell all his commerce, pick up his cross and come follow him. If God can ever get our hearts, then everything else will follow suit. The heart is the seat of our emotions and is the origin of our thoughts and our intent. There are three things that Jesus tells the man to do and each one is an action toward obedience. First, the rich ruler was to sell his resources and give them to the poor. I believe this would be a struggle for 90 percent of the world because money is a sturdy support system for us to lean on. The second deals with overcoming our fleshly desires. When we get entangled with the world and embrace what it has to offer, our footsteps in following the King become less frequent. It takes the discipline of a mature believer and the innocence of a young child to obey. Finally, the man was commanded by Jesus to follow Him. In other words, be His disciple.

Imagine being sought out by the Master of the universe to do magnanimous work for the kingdom. To walk with the Word of Truth and be an eyewitness to a myriad of miracles. To hear the dynamic and the devoted words that fell from the Master's mouth that destroyed the yoke of bondage in the believer's life. To glean and grab hold of the perfect character of God that made the demons afraid. How many of us would jump at this opportunity? Well, when we surrender our will and allow the Spirit of God to have His way in our life, it is just like Jesus commanded us to follow Him.

For we are His workmanship, created in Christ Jesus unto good works, which God hath before ordained that we should walk in them.

— (Ephesians 2:10 KJV)

For this man to obey the words of Jesus, he needed to have a regenerated heart. What I mean is that the heart of man is callous to the things of God, for we are at enmity with the rule of His authority. It is only when our heart is changed from a heart of stone to that of flesh we can walk with Him. Our emotion is married to the world and therefore, hangs out in that affiliation which is the antithesis of God's plan for our life. In 1 Samuel 24:6, we see the regenerated heart of David.

It says that the world looks at life through a different lens. Therefore, it acquiesces to follow in the footsteps of the flesh. But David, the man after God's own heart, had the opportunity to kill the man standing in the way of his success. The Bible puts it this way, David settled it in his heart that he would wait until God removed his adversary so that he would have entry to what the Lord had purposed for him. A regenerated heart directs and navigates our decision-making so that God's perfect will is being manifested for His glory. What is often left out but is a necessary part of the equation is having a renewed mind. The mind plays a major part in having the mental faculties fully active to address the subject at hand. In spiritual matters, it is to be fully engaged to glean the spiritual truths from God and gravitate to His command to perform.

The Apostle Paul writes to the believer that we should not conform to the thinking of the world but be transformed by the renewed mind that has been seared in us by God's Spirit. J. B. Phillips gives us a paraphrase of Romans 12:2, "Don't let the world around you squeeze you into its own mold." In layman's terms, as Christians, we should abandon the lifestyle and the logistics of how the world functions. One way is to let love be without dissimulation or disguised. Let your love be shed abroad, having no deceptive marks, no hang-ups and no boundaries. The struggle comes when the world system begins to feed our flesh, which causes us to be tossed and turned by every new thing. As a result, we become bound by the decrees and the doctrine that dictates our surroundings.

The rich ruler could not get past the idea of Jesus pushing him to give up something that he treasured so much, not understanding that what God had for him was far more valuable. Many of us are in the same camp as the rich ruler, for we have a closed fist when it comes to the concept of giving. When I was a restaurant manager, I struggled with the idea of sampling. My rationale was how can I maximize my bottom line if I am giving something away? What I had overlooked was the missing denominator, which was the love for the customer. By letting unpaying customers taste my product, I was sensitive to their needs in how they would spend their money. At the same time, I invited them to purchase my product several times over. The Lord was working on the rich ruler's mind, getting him to see that love was the missing denominator in his receiving everlasting life. Money can come and go, for it is temporal but the life of a person is priceless and their soul is eternal.

The Call

Jesus had a plan for this man and it involved a great work before he would enter into the gates of heaven. Can you imagine being in the company of Jesus and soaking up all that wisdom? Being on the front line as an eyewitness to all the miracles that were ministered to those who needed healing. The Lord Jesus was extending this man the opportunity to be one of His disciples. It is the Greek word *mathetes*, which comes over into English as a learner or pupil. The disciple was one who walked behind the teacher and wrote down everything that was said but also took on the physical duties of an apprentice.

Having a platform to speak boldly to the masses about your faith, for you once sat at the feet of the Master. I know the thoughts that would pass through my mind would be endless. This beautiful soul, who claimed that he kept the law, needed that Bright Light to shine down in his soul, which housed his conscience and his convictions. After being in Jesus's presence and having the word of truth deposited in his spirit, he should have been convinced to carry the mantle of the Christian faith, much like Abraham. The prophet Isaiah was one who experienced this great light from God, known as the *Shekinah Glory*. In the first five chapters of the book of Isaiah, we are told of his hardship and his becoming weary from the cares of this world. In chapter one, it speaks of the continuous sins of the people. (Isaiah 1:2-20 KJV) In chapter two, God speaks to the people of their impending judgment coming in their future. (Isaiah 2:6-22 KJV) In chapter three, a coming leadership crisis. (Isaiah 3:1-15 KJV)

Chapter five, a love song goes sour. (Isaiah 5:1-7 KJV) When we get to chapter six, the faithfulness of God finds Isaiah and ushers him into the temple, where he sees that Light, the Lamb of God, sitting on His throne. This is what the prophet needed to see, authentic worship given to the *Agnus Dei*, which would give him refreshment and reinvigoration to continue to minister in excellence.

The Affectual Weight Of The World

Here is the perception, whenever you leave the presence of God, you also leave yourself vulnerable to the imperfections and the deficiencies of the world. This rich ruler who once ran to Jesus now walks away from the Lord of Glory. The biblical truth is that you never stay in a neutral position after being in the company of Jesus. You will either be on fire for God or your soul will become more callous and colder for the things of the Kingdom. The rich ruler walked away because he loved the world more than the thing that he was seeking answers for. How important it is to know Jesus and not have a superficial understanding of the power of God. Standing in this man's presence was the author and the restorer of life. What the rich ruler did not understand was that the Creator God, who asked him to give away his riches, had the power to restore and replenish everything he released one hundred-fold. Looking at it from the scope of a humanistic point of view, most of us would have behaved just as the rich ruler. We would have wrestled in our minds to be obedient or to disobey Jesus and ask for forgiveness down the road. As season believers, we should strive to operate in the *Coram Deo*, to live in the face of God.

The Apostle John tells us that we are not to fall in love with the world, for it will cause us to spurn God's agenda for our life. The things of God are not compatible with the world system, whose desire is to operate separately from God's authority. The world gets its cue from the lust of the flesh, the lust of the eyes and the pride of life. Notice that all three are independent and do not rely on God's power to transform nor transcend any value in you. The lust of the flesh refers to the bodily appetite that stems from our evil nature. The lust of the eyes germinates from what our physical eyes see. The pride of life relates to our unholy ambition to store up vainglory. When these three components are your foundation, it puts you on a collision course of receiving the blessing of God and being attracted to a world system that is fading away. The lust for anything is a desperate act that defies love and is the great misnomer for every heart that yields something to love.

The Flickering Light

At this the man's face fell. He went away sad, because he had great wealth.

— Mark 10:22 NIV

What a sad commentary that will be raked over how we mismanaged our accounts in the eyes of God. We wasted the riches that He had placed in our hands and it resulted in an unprofitable return. As the rich ruler fades into the crowd, it paints a portrait of the turbulence of life. One minute you have happy feet and the hope of hearing good news awaits you. Moments later, meditating on the response that wrecks your joy-bells. This man, who had money and was standing in the presence of light, disappears while the flickering torch is about to be distinguished in his life. What a vivid image for the people of that day to witness, for they whole heartily believed that riches were associated with blessings and favor from God.

Is this not how we view the well-off and the wealthy in our society? That they are endowed with God's unmerited favor and His hand of provisions rests solely on them. Proverbs 10:15 says that the rich man's wealth is his strong city and the destruction of the poor is their poverty. In essence, what is being conveyed is that the rich get richer and the poor go into poverty. The rich have the resources to make money while the poor do not have the means to get started. Mary Church Terrell, one of the great leaders of the women's civil rights movement, put it this way, "We must lift as we climb." Terrell was addressing the responsibility of one reaching back and pulling up the person next to you as you scale the walls of success. She relates that reaching back could come in the form of mentoring, facilitating and addressing people's needs. The Bible teaches us that we are blessed to be a blessing and that we are not to horde the gifts from God for our own benefit.

With Empty Hands We Walk Into Eternity

Jesus makes the promise that everyone who forsakes all for His name's sake will have great rewards in the present day and in eternity. It was once said that a blessed man is one who has his hands open so that God has the liberty to take out and put back in. This is a word picture that affirms our faith. It is the hinge by which the doors of eternity are open to us. Why should we waver in our hearts to trust that bright light? In Christ Jesus, we have everything we need if we just believe. Be confident in that inner man who has his faith in God, the one who knows the end from the beginning. The Lord of Glory has fortified you with the determination to walk with boldness, not with reckless abandonment. But to have the resolve to commit to what God has decreed for you to accomplish.

For I know the plans I have for you," declares the LORD, "plans to prosper you and and not to harm you, plans to give you hope and a future."

— Jeremiah:29:11 NIV

He has shaped and molded you for greatness and has set you apart to do spectacular and supernatural work. God will not withhold anything from you that will prohibit nor prolong His desired will for your life. Making your faith active is a motivator that moves God to act on your behalf. When you walk with Him, you will experience His power that has been unleashed and will provide you with unlimited resources that will put you on the winning side of your destiny. Hold firm to the thought that your destiny is not your ending but the place for your new beginning. It is the watershed moment that ushers in refreshment and rest for greater days ahead. This process starts when you open your hands and come to Jesus, withholding nothing.

The Gospel

In the economy of God, the gospel is essential, for it is His good news. It is God calling you out of darkness into His marvelous light. It is the faithfulness of the Father who sends the Son to rescue those who are rich in earthly goods but poor in heavenly treasures. Luther said it best when he penned this allegory, "The soul of Christ has two eyes. He has a right eye and a left eye. The right eye focuses in on the full intuition of the perfect existence of the things in heaven, while the left eye focuses in on man and his fallen carnality. So, Christ the God-man was called to restore the broken relationship between the right eye and the left eye."

God will use everything at His disposal to win you to Himself. In His providence, His long-suffering displays how He waits and waits for you and me to partake in a Father-to-child relationship. His desire is that no one would perish nor be dismissed from His presence. How Jesus must have felt the heaviness of rejection as the rich young ruler disappeared into the crowd. Jesus communicates the good news to the crowd of that day and to us who want to know what is needed to have eternal life. God was not displaying His lack of *agape* love towards the rich young ruler by not opening the doors of salvation to him.

God must remain just in everything that He does to be holy. God gives men and women the opportunity to walk through the doors of eternity when we come by faith, believing in His perfect plan to redeem. Salvation is a divine work that is proclaimed by God, obtained by God and sustained by God. It is a work done by God alone.

> Jesus said to them, *"My Father is always at His work to this very day, and I too am working."*
>
> *— John 5:17 NIV*

Today is always a good day to have that conversation with Jesus. His bright light is always shining and ready to receive you.

A Prayer To The Reader

Heavenly Father, I pray that the story of the rich young ruler has sparked a willingness in someone's spirit to take inventory of where they stand in Your presence. May their heart yield to the commands of the Lord, and their mind be open to hearing the voice of the Savior calling them unto Himself. I ask that You will forgive everyone of their sins and renew their spirit with the righteousness of Jesus. In Jesus name, Amen.

Romans Road Pathway To Salvation

Romans 3:23 *For all have sinned, and come short of the glory of the glory of God.*

Romans 6:23 *For the wages of sin is death; but the gift of God is eternal life through Jesus Christ our Lord.*

Romans 5:8 *But God demonstrates his own love for us in this: While we were still sinners, Christ died for us.*

Romans 10:9 *That if thou shall confess with thy mouth the Lord Jesus, and believe in thine heart that God hath raised him from the dead, thou shall be saved.*

Romans 10:10 *For with the heart man believeth unto righteousness; and with the mouth confession*

Bibliography

1. https://www.bibletools.org/index.cfm/fuseaction/Bible.show/sVerseID/28248/eVerseID/28249/version/ISV, Romans 12:2 (ISV) - Forerunner Commentary

2. Bible Study Pro.com: Greek Dictionary.

3. Bibles: The King James Bible, The New King James, New International Version, New Life Version, The American Standard Bible

4. *Creation Ex Nihilo by R.C. Sproul from Foundations: An Overview of Systematic Theology.* (n.d.). [Video]. Ligonier Ministries. https://www.ligonier.org/learn/series/foundations/creation-ex-nihilo

5. D. E. Gregory: Prayer & Promises for Men; Broad Street Publishing, Savage, Minnesota, copyright 2020.

6. Favor Definition & Meaning | Dictionary.com. https://www.dictionary.com/browse/favor

7. "Johannes Kepler." *New World Encyclopedia,* . 1 Aug 2022, 15:06 UTC. 25 Mar 2023, 19:46 <https://www.newworldencyclopedia.org/p/index.php?title=Johannes_Kepler&oldid=1074927>.

8. Michael Rydelnik, Michael Vanlaningham, Louis A. Barbieri, Michael Boyle, James Coakley: The Moody Bible Commentary; Moody Publishers, Chicago, IL, copyright 1984.

9. Paul Johnson: The History of the Jews; Harper Collins, Amazon.com, copyright 2009.

10. *Some of the Dopest Black Women You've Never Heard Of.* (2017, March 30). Retrieved March 27, 2023, from https://shoppeblack.us/tag/national-association-of-colored-women/

11. The Septuagint version: Greek and English, Regency Reference Library/Zondervan Pub. House, year 1986

12. William MacDonald: Believer's Bible Commentary; Thomas Nelson Publishers, Nashville, Tennessee, copyright 1995.

13. *The Talmud.* Reform Judaism. (n.d.). Retrieved April 1, 2023, from https://reformjudaism.org/talmud

Bibliography

14. Mishnayot-Six Orders of the Mishnah. (n.d.). https://www.chabad.org/library/article_cdo/aid/5689767/jewish/Mishnah.htm. Retrieved]\April 1, 2023, from
https://www.chabad.org/library/article_cdo/aid/5689767/jewish/Mishnah.htm

15. All references from *City of God* are from Saint Augustine, *The City of God* Translated by Henry Betterson. (London: Penguin Books, 1984)

16. JDS Christ Media. (2020, August 14). *Martin Luther | full movie in English | #martinLuther #jdschristmedia* [Video]. YouTube. Retrieved April 5, 2023, from https://www.youtube.com/watch?v=C8x-mKwfc9k

17. *Martin Luther | Encyclopedia.com*. (n.d.). https://www.encyclopedia.-com/people/philosophy-and-religion/protestant-christianity-biographies/martin-luther

18. *The Theologia Germanica of Martin Luther*. (1980, January). [Video]. https://books.google.com/

19. *Don't be conformed to the world | Forging Bonds*. (n.d.). https://www.forgingbonds.org/blog/detail/how-christians-are-squeezed-into-the-cultures-mold

20. Gertz, S., Williams, D. H., & McGuckin, J. (2005). *Debating Jesus Divinity: Did you know?*https://christianhistoryinstitute.org/uploaded/50cf8890789f-b9.66364599.pdf. Retrieved April 17, 2023, from https://christianhistoryinstitute.org/uploaded/50cf8890789fb9.66364599.pdf